The Mausoleum Of Halicarnassus...

James Fergusson

THE

MAUSOLEUM AT HALICARNASSUS

RESTORED

IN CONFORMITY WITH

THE RECENTLY DISCOVERED REMAINS.

BY JAMES FERGUSSON,

FELLOW ROYAL INSTITUTE OF BRITISH ARCHITECTS.
AUTHOR OF THE 'HANDBOOK OF ARCHITECTURE;' 'ESSAY ON THE TOPOGRAPHY OF JERUSALEM,' &c.

LONDON:
JOHN MURRAY, ALBEMARLE STREET.
1862.

LONDON : PRINTED BY WILLIAM CLOWES AND SONS, STAMFORD STREET,
AND CHARING CROSS.

PREFACE.

THE Essay contained in the following pages has no pretension to being a complete account of the Mausoleum at Halicarnassus. All that has been attempted in the present instance is to recapitulate and explain the various data which have recently been brought to light for restoring that celebrated monument of antiquity; and to show in what manner these may be applied so as to perfect a solution of the riddle which has so long perplexed the student of classical architecture.

At some future period it may be worth while to go more fully and with more careful elaboration into the whole subject; but to do this as it should be done, would require more leisure and better opportunities than are at present at the Author's disposal for such a purpose.

20, LANGHAM PLACE,

May, 1862.

CONTENTS.

PAGE.

INTRODUCTION   5

CHAPTER I.

SCRIPTA   8

RELIQUIÆ   12

EXEMPLA   14

RATIONES   16

CHAPTER II.

GREEK MEASURES   20

CYMATIUM   22

PTERON   24

PYRAMID   27

VERTICAL HEIGHTS   30

ARCHITECTURAL ORDINANCE   33

LACUNARIA   36

SCULPTURE AND PEDESTALS   38

CONCLUSION   43

LIST OF WOODCUTS.

1. LION TOMB, CNIDUS   14

2. TOMB AT DUGGA   15

3. TOMB AT MYLASSA   16

4. CYMATIUM   22

5. SECTION OF CYMATIUM AND OF BASE OF PYRAMID   29

6. PEDESTAL OF MONTE CAVALLO GROUP   41

DIRECTION TO BINDER.

Place *Plates* I., II., and III. at the end of the work.

MAUSOLEUM AT HALICARNASSUS.

INTRODUCTION.

OF all the examples of the wonderful arts of the Greeks, the remains or the memories of which have come down to us, no one has excited such curiosity as the far-famed Mausoleum at Halicarnassus, or such regret that no fragments of it should have existed in our own days. All we knew of it, till very recently, was that the ancients themselves were inclined to look upon it as the very best specimen of architectural art which they possessed. For not only did they rank it as among the seven wonders of the world, but assigned it that pre-eminence—not because of its size or durability, but because of the intrinsic beauty of its design, and the mode in which it was ornamented.

The Pyramids of Egypt and Walls of Babylon were wonders only because of their mass or their durability. The Palace of Cyrus or the Hanging Gardens of Babylon may have been rich in colour and barbaric splendour, but we know enough of Assyrian and of Persian art to feel convinced that the taste in which they were designed must at least have been very questionable. The Colossus at Rhodes, and the Statue of Jupiter at Elis, whatever their merits,—and of one, at least, of them we can believe anything,—did not belong to architectural art. The Temple of Ephesus may have been beautiful in itself, but it became a wonder only from its size, as the largest of Greek temples. But the Mausoleum, which covered not more than one-sixth or one-seventh of its area, could have been remarkable only because it was beautiful, or in consequence of the elaboration and taste displayed in its ornamentation.

All that was known of this once celebrated building, till the recent explorations, was to be gathered from a few laudatory paragraphs in Pausanias, Strabo, Vitruvius, and other authors of that age; and a description in Pliny's Natural History, which we are now justified in assuming to have been abstracted from a work written by the architects who originally designed the Mausoleum itself. Probably there were no diagrams or illustrations with their book, and we may suspect that Pliny himself did not understand the building he undertook to describe. At all events, it is certain that he stated its peculiarities in such a manner as to be utterly unintelligible to future generations.

Still there were so many facts in his statements, and the building was so celebrated, that few architects have escaped the temptation of trying to restore it. What the squaring of the circle is to the young mathematician, or the perpetual motion to the young mechanician, the Mausoleum at Halicarnassus was to the young architect; and with the data at his disposal this problem seemed as insoluble as the other two.

Some forty or fifty of these restorations have been published, and a strange and amusing collection they are. Some are round, some octagonal, some cruciform, some oblong or square in plan, some are squat, some tall.* Every dimension found in Pliny was applied to every part in succession, but in vain. All these designs had only one thing in common;—that they were all wrong, —some more, some less so, but none seizing what now turn out to be the main features of the design.

In 1846, Lord Stratford de Redcliffe, who was then all-powerful as our ambassador at Constantinople, obtained from the Porte a firman for the removal of certain bassi-rilievi which had been built into the walls of the Castle of Budrum, the ancient Halicarnassus. These arrived in England in due course, and were at once admitted to be fragments of the sculpture of the Mausoleum, as it had been previously assumed that they were. But their beauty only served further to increase the regret that all traces of the building to which they once belonged should have been, as it then appeared, for ever lost.

While things were in this very unsatisfactory position, the public heard with no small degree of interest that Mr. Charles Newton, formerly one of the officers of the British Museum, and then Vice-Consul at Mitylene, had not only discovered the true site of the Mausoleum on a spot formerly indicated by Professor Donaldson, but had found considerable remains of the long-lost building.

Public attention was still further attracted to the subject when it was announced that the British Government had fitted out an extensive expedition, to continue the explorations commenced by Mr. Newton at Budrum and its neighbourhood. From the time that the expeditionary force commenced its labours in October, 1856, till it was broken up nearly three years afterwards, in June, 1859, occasional paragraphs kept up the interest in its proceedings, and latterly the arrival of the marbles themselves excited expectation to the highest pitch. Everything seemed to shadow forth a most brilliant success; and, from the high character which Mr. Newton bore as a Greek scholar, and a thoroughly educated archæologist, all the Hellenist public rejoiced that an expedition fitted out on so liberal a scale, and for so desirable an object, had fallen into what all then believed to be such competent hands.

---

* Of this class one of the best known is the steeple of St. George's Church, Bloomsbury, which its architect supposed was a correct restoration of the Mausoleum.

The first published results were not encouraging. They took the form of Papers presented to Parliament, and published as a Blue Book in 1858, and a second series entitled " Further Papers relating to the Excavations at Budrum and Cnidus, presented in August, 1859."

The diagrams of the Mausoleum which accompanied these Papers seemed only sufficient to prove one of two things ;—either that the explorations had not resulted in the discovery of a sufficient quantity of architectural forms to enable a satisfactory restoration to be made, or that those who conducted the expedition were not sufficiently versed in the art of putting together architectural fragments to be able to avail themeslves of the information that had been obtained.

The whole results of the expedition were at last laid before the public in February last, in a folio volume of plates accompanied by a volume of text in 8vo. by Mr. Newton. This work contains, among other things, an elaborate restoration of the Mausoleum by Mr. Pullan, an architect who was sent out by the Trustees of the British Museum to join the expedition during the continuance of its labours. This restoration, however, turns out on examination to be less satisfactory than those previously published by Lieut. Smith in the parliamentary papers above alluded to, either as a specimen of Greek art or as a solution of the difficulties inherent in the problem of reconciling the recent discoveries with the ancient descriptions of the building. It is also unfortunate that—owing probably to their author being absent from the country—the purely architectural plates are so incorrectly drawn or engraved as to add considerably to the previously existing difficulties of the question. It is likewise to be regretted that, for some reason which is not explained, all the best things are omitted from the collection. The statue of Mausolus is not there, nor that of the Goddess which accompanied the chariot. The Horses of the Chariot are also omitted; so is the Torso of the prancing Amazon, the finest thing found ; so are the Castle bassi-rilievi, and the really fine Lions. There are, in fact, materials left out sufficient to fill, if not so large a volume as the present, at least one of a far higher class. Notwithstanding these difficulties and defects, there appear to be sufficient materials now before the public to effect a restoration of the building, and as almost all that was discovered on the spot is now in the British Museum, a reference to them enables us to correct or verify what has been published. Under these circumstances I have not hesitated to make the attempt. With what success I must leave it to others to judge after a perusal of the contents of the following pages.

CHAPTER I.

THE materials which now exist for restoring the Mausoleum are of four different kinds. These are :—

First.—The passages in various ancient authors which either describe the appearance of the building or give its dimensions.

Secondly.—The actual remains of the building discovered in the recent explorations, and the measurements of the ground then obtained.

Thirdly.—The several tombs existing in Asia and Africa, evidently of the same type, and which afford valuable hints for the restoration.

Lastly.—The system of definite proportions in Greek architecture, which is not only most useful in suggesting forms, but also most valuable in rectifying deductions arrived at from other sources.

1. *Scripta.*

Among the things written with regard to the Mausoleum, by far the most important is the celebrated passage in Pliny's Natural History.* It is to the following effect : " Scopas had, as rivals in the same age, Bryaxis, and Timotheus, and Leochares, who should be mentioned together, as they were equally employed in the sculptures of the Mausoleum, a sepulchre erected by his wife Artemisia to Mausolus, King of Caria, who died in the second year of the hundred and seventh Olympiad. It was mainly owing to the work of the above-named artists that this building was considered one of the seven wonders of the world. It extends on the north and south 63 feet, but is shorter on the other fronts. The whole circumference is 411 feet. It is raised in height 25 cubits, and is surrounded by 36 columns. This part was called the pteron. The sculptures on the east side were by Scopas, on the north by Bryaxis, on the south by Timotheus, and on the west by Leochares. Before they had finished

---

* xxxvi. v. " Scopas habuit æmulos eadem ætate Bryaxim et Timotheum et Leocharen, de quibus simul dicendum est, quoniam pariter cœlavere Mausoleum ; sepulchrum hoc est ab uxore Artemisia factum Mausolo Cariæ regulo, qui obiit Olympiadis cvii anno secundo : opus id ut esset inter septem miracula, hi maxime fecere artifices. Patet ab austro et septemtrione sexagenos ternos pedes, brevius a frontibus, toto circuitu pedes quadringentos undecim ; attollitur in altitudinem viginti quinque cubitis ; cingitur columnis triginta sex ; pteron vocavere circuitum. Ab oriente cœlavit Scopas, a septentrione Bryaxis, a meridie Timotheus, ab occasu Leochares, priusque quam peragerent regina obiit ; non tamen recesserunt nisi absoluto jam, id gloriæ ipsorum artisque monimentum judicantes ; hodieque certant manus. Accessit et quintus artifex ; namque supra pteron pyramis altitudine inferiorem æquavit, viginti quatuor gradibus in metæ cacumen se contrahens. In summo est quadriga marmorea, quam fecit Pythis ; hæc adjecta centum quadraginta pedum altitudine totum opus includit."

their work, the Queen Artemisia, who had ordered this building to be constructed in honour of her husband's memory, died ; but they did not on that account cease from their labours till it was entirely finished, regarding it as a monument of their own fame and of art ; and to this day the work testifies to their rivalry in merit.   A fifth artist was joined to them ; for above the pteron there was a pyramid equal in height to the lower part, with 24 steps, contracting into a summit, like that of a meta.   On the top of all this was a quadriga in marble, made by Pythis.   These being added, the height of the whole work was equal to 140 feet."

It is easy to see what difficulties were involved in this description.   How, in the first instance, was it possible that a building which was only 63 feet in length in plan, and shorter on the other sides, could be 411 feet in circumference ? and, in regard to height, what substantive was to be supplied after "inferiorem"?   If "partem," it might apply to the pteron, which is the only part mentioned in the previous description ; but the logic seemed to require "pyramidem," and if so, what was it ?   If either, how was the whole height of 140 feet to be made up ?

In looking a little carefully into the matter we can now guess how it was that Pliny came to state these dimensions in so enigmatical a manner ; for we learn from Vitruvius * that Satyrus and Phytheus, two of the architects employed in the building, wrote a description of their work, which no doubt Pliny had access to ; but as he was thinking more of the sculpture than of the architecture, he jotted down these dimensions without probably realising the form of the building himself, and left them as a bewildering enigma for posterity.   Now that we have the means of verifying them, these figures are ten times more valuable than the most vivid description of the general appearance of the building would be to us ; but it is only now that we feel this.

The only other author who furnishes us with any dimensions is Hyginus, a grammarian in the time of Augustus.   In enumerating the seven wonders of the world, he describes the "Monument of King Mausolus, built of shining (?) (*lychnicis*) stones, 80 feet in height, and 1340 feet in circumference."   Neither of these dimensions agrees with Pliny's ; but the latter evidently refers to the peribolus, the wall of which was found in the recent excavations.†   The former, for reasons to be given hereafter, I fancy should be 80 *cubits*, meaning thereby Halicarnassian or Babylonian cubits of 21 inches each.   If so, it is Pliny's exact dimension ; but the matter is not important, as the text of Hyginus is avowedly so corrupt, and he is of such low repute, that his assertion is of little importance in the controversy.

Vitruvius unfortunately adds very little to our knowledge of the building.

---

* vii. Pref.
† The dimensions of the walls of this peribolus, as found in these excavations, accord with tolerable accuracy with those here given.

C

He describes its situation as in the centre of the curve formed by the town, encircling its bay like a theatre, and with a broad street, "*platea*," leading from the *agora* on the shore up to the Mausoleum.[*] He adds, " Mausoleum ita egregiis operibus est factum ;" from which we may infer, as in fact we do from all other descriptions, that the building was more remarkable for its sculpture and its details than for its dimensions.

Among the Greek authors, the most amusing account is that given by Lucian in his ' Dialogues of the Dead.' He there makes Mausolus say, in reply to the scoffing inquiry of Diogenes (after recounting his exploits), " Besides that personal superiority, I am beautiful, tall of stature, and of so robust a constitution as enabled me to sustain all the hardships and fatigues of war ; but, to be brief, the principal point is, I have a prodigious monument raised over me at Halicarnassus, which for magnitude and beauty has not its equal in the whole world. It is decorated with the most exquisite figures of men and horses, all carried to such a degree of perfection, and in such exceedingly fine marbles, as you will not easily find even in a Temple." Further on, Diogenes remarks, " As to your monument and the costly marble of which it is built, the inhabitants of Halicarnassus may certainly have reason to show it to strangers, and to think much of themselves for possessing so costly a work within their walls ; but, my handsome friend, I do not see what sort of enjoyment you should have in it. You should only say that you bear a heavier load than the rest of us, since you have such an enormous heap of stones lying on you ! "

The few words found in Pausanias add little to our knowledge, but serve to show the estimation in which the Mausoleum was held. He says, " Although there are many sepulchres worthy of admiration, two may especially be mentioned ; one at Halicarnassus, the other that of Helena of Adiabene at Jerusalem." With regard to the first he adds, " It was erected for Mausolus, who reigned at Halicarnassus, and was so wonderful, not only on account of the magnitude of the work, but also from the magnificence of its ornaments, that the Romans considered it among the wonders of the world, and called all their most magnificent tombs *mausolea*, after it."[†]

Strabo merely mentions that it was considered one of the wonders of the world.

From this time to that of its final demolition by the Knights of St. John between 1402 and 1522 A.D., the Mausoleum is mentioned as still standing by Gregory of Nazianzum in the fourth century, and later by Nicetus of Cappadocia and by Constantine Porphyrogenitus in the tenth century ; but the most important fact is the mention of it by Eustathius, two centuries afterwards, who, in his commentary on the ' Iliad,' says of the Mausoleum, that " it was *and is* a wonder."[‡]

---

[*] Vitruvius, II. viii. 37 and 37.   [†] Pausanias, viii. 16.   [‡] Newton, page 73.

From all this we are justified in assuming that down to the twelfth century
the Mausoleum was at least sufficiently perfect to convey a correct idea of its
original magnificence.   Between this period and the year 1402, when the city
was taken possession of by the Knights of St. John, we are led to infer that the
building must have been ruined, most probably by the shock of an earthquake,—
the position of many of the fragments found being such as to be explicable only
on such an hypothesis.

The Knights, it seems, immediately set about erecting the present Castle,
and the remains of the Mausoleum supplied not only stone, but lime for the
building.   Still the materials were far from being exhausted by this process in
the first instance, for in 1472 Cepio mentions the remains as remarkable, and a
certain Coriolanus speaks of them with more marked admiration.   By far the
most detailed account, however, is found in the following extract from Guichard's
' Funerailles des Rommains,' printed at Lyons, 1581, and for which, as for all
the above mediæval information, we are indebted to the researches of Mr.
Newton, from whose work I have abstracted it.   The passage runs as follows in
the old French, and is quoted entire, as it is almost as important to the
restoration of the monument as that of Pliny itself :—

"L'an 1522, lors que Sultan Solyman se préparoit pour venir assaillir les Rhodiens, le
Grand Maistre sçachāt l'importance de ceste place, et que le Turc ne faudrait point de
l'empieter de premiere abordee, s'il pouuoit, y ennoya quelques cheualiers pour la remparer
et mettre ordre à tout ce qui estoit necessaire soustenir l'ennemi, du nombre desquels fut le
Commandeur de la Tourette Lyonnois, lequel se treuua depuis à la prise de Rhodes, et vint
en France, où il fit, de ce que ie vay dire maintenāt, le recit à Monsieur d'Alechamps,
personnage assez recognu par ses doctes escrits, et que ie nomme seulement à fin qu'on
sçache de qui ie tien vne histoire si remarcable.   Ces cheualiers estans arriués à Mesy,
se mirent incontinent en deuoir de faire fortifier le chasteau, et pour auoir de la chaux, ne
treuuans pierre aux enuirons plus propre pour en cuire, ni qui leur vinst plus aisee, que
certaines marches de marbre blanc, qui s'esleuoyent en forme de perron emmy d'un champ
près du port, là où iadis estoit la grande place d'Halycarnasse, ils les firēt abattre et
prendre pour cest effect.   La pierre s'estant rencōtree bonne, fut cause, que ce peu de
maçonnerie, qui parroissoit sur terre, ayant esté demoli, ils firent fouiller plus bas en
esperance d'en treuuer d'auantage.   Ce qui leur succeda fort heureusement : car ils
recognurent en peu d'heure, que de tant plus qu'on creusoit profond, d'autant plus
s'eslargissoit par le bas la fabrique, qui leur fournit par apres de pierres, non seulement
à faire de la chaux, mais aussi pour bastir.   Au bout de quatre ou cinque iours, apres
auoir faict vne grande descouuerte, par vne apres disnee ils virent ouuerture comme pour
entrer dans vne caue : ils prirent de la chandelle, et deualerent dedans, où ils treuuerent
vne belle grande salle carree, embellie tout au tour de colonnes de marbre, avec leur
bases, chapiteaux, architraues, frises et cornices grauees et taillees en demy bosse :
l'entredeux des colonnes estait reuestu de lastres, listeaux ou plattes bandes de marbre
de diuerses couleurs ornees de moulures et sculptures conformes au reste de l'œuure, et
rapportés propermēt sur le fonds blāc de la muraille, où ne se voyait qu'histoires
taillees, et toutes battailles à demy relief.   Ce qu'ayans admiré de prime face, et apres
auoir estimé en leur fantāsie la singularite de l'ouurage, en fin ils defirent, briserent, et
rompirent, pour s'en seruir comme ils auoyent faicte du demeurant.   Outre ceste sale ils
treuuerent apres vne porte fort basse, qui conduisoit à une autre, comme antichambre, ou

il y auoit vn sepulcre auec son vase et son tymbre de marbre blanc, fort beau et reluisant
à merueilles, lequel, pour n'avoir pas eu assez de temps, ils ne descouurirent, la retraicte
estant desia sonnee.   Le lendemain, apres qu'ils y furent retournés, ils treuuerēt la tombe
descouuerte, et la terre semee autour de force petits morceaux de drap d'or, et paillette de
mesme metal : qu leur fit penser, que les corsaires, qui escumoyent alors le long de toute
ceste coste, ayans eu quelque vent de ce qui auoit esté descouuert en ce lieu là, y vindrent
de nuict, et osterent le couuercle du sepulcre, et tient on qu'ils y treuuerent des grandes
richesses et thresors.   Ainsi ce superbe sepulcre, compté pour l'un des sept miracles, et
ouurages merueilleux du monde, apres auoir eschappé la fureur des Barbares, et demeuré
l'espace de 2247 ans debout, du moins enseueli dedans les ruines de la ville d'Halycarnasse,
fut descouuert et aboli pour remparer le chasteau de S. Pierre, par les cheualiers croisés de
Rhodes, lesquels en furent incontinent apres chassés par le Turc, et de toute l'Asie quant
et quant."

The demolition at that period seems to have been nearly complete, though
it is probable that from that time to this, the Turks may have been in the habit
of using such blocks of marble as may have remained above ground, to make
lime.   At all events, so completely was all trace of it above ground obliterated,
that even so experienced an observer as Captain Spratt failed, after the most
minute survey of the neighbourhood, to fix on the site where this wonder of the
world had once stood.

2. *Reliquiæ.*

The one redeeming point in the conduct of these barbarian Knights was
that, instead of burning all the sculptures into lime, they built some thirteen
slabs of one of the friezes, and some of the lions, into the walls of their castle.
These had early attracted the attention of travellers, and a view of them *in situ*
was published by the Dilettante Society in their second volume of 'Ionian
Antiquities' in 1797.   In 1846, Lord Stratford de Redcliffe obtained a
firman for their removal, and they were sent home to the British Museum in
Her Majesty's ship *Siren*.

Nothing further was done till the explorations commenced, as before
mentioned, by Mr. Newton, in 1855, and the establishment of the expedition
there in the following year ; though, from various causes, it was not till the 1st
of January, 1857, that they were really able to commence excavations on the
site of the Mausoleum.

The principal discoveries which rewarded their exertions were :—

First.—Some thirty or forty blocks which formed part of the steps of the
pyramid mentioned by Pliny.   These all (with two exceptions) showed, by the
weather marks on their upper surface, that they had been constructed of two
breadths only—the tread, or upper exposed part of the steps, being always
either 1 ft. 5 in. or 1 ft. 9 in. English, according to Messrs. Smith, Pullan, or
Newton.   The real dimension, however, as we shall see presently, was probably in inches and decimals of an inch 17·01 and 21·2526.

Even more important than these were four or five angle-stones of the
pyramid, showing the same dimensions in juxtaposition on their two faces.   It is

much to be regretted that the exact number of these stones which were found was not noted. If there had been three, and they had all been found together, which seems to have been the case, they might,—probably would,—all have belonged to one course. With four this is less probable, but it still leaves it open to any one who has a theory such as that of Mr. Cockerell or Mr. Falkener, or who might suggest a curvilinear one (as I once did), to assert that this was so, and thus leave the whole question still in doubt. If there were five this would be impossible, and it would simplify the argument to a considerable extent.

The truth of the matter seems to be that Lieutenant Smith's business there was to take charge of the Sappers and Miners under his command ; Mr. Newton was only anxious to procure specimens of sculpture for the National Museum ; and before Mr. Pullan arrived, a great deal that had been discovered was covered up again and no record left. Many points that might then have been easily cleared up must now, therefore, be left in doubt, unless some one will take the trouble of doing over again what has been so carelessly done once.

Secondly.—Almost equally important with these were some portions of the cymatium of the order. Like the greater steps, this was composed of pieces, 21 inches in length, and on each alternate one, covering the joint, was a lion's head—thus 3 ft. 6 in. apart from centre to centre. From this we get, with almost absolute certainty, the width of the intercolumniations as twice, thrice, or four times 3 ft. 6 in.

Thirdly.—A capital and base of a column, very nearly perfect were found, and fragments of several others ;—a considerable number of frustra of the columns and fragments of the architrave and cornice. The frieze we assume that we knew before from the sculptures already in the Museum. In fact, a sufficient number of fragments were recovered to enable us to restore the whole " order " with very tolerable approximative certainty. All these parts are more or less chipped and broken, so that minute differences still exist ; but on the whole we may feel tolerably certain that it reached, as nearly as may be, the height of 25 cubits or 37 ft. 6 in. Greek, mentioned by Pliny.

Fourthly.—Some stones of the lacunaria of the roof were found, but not in a sufficiently perfect state to enable us to be certain of any dimensions from them. Mr. Pullan makes them fit an intercolumniation of 10 feet,—Professor Cockerell, it is understood, applies them to one of 8·75; and they would be found equally applicable to various other dimensions.

Fifthly.—No other strictly architectural fragments were found, but portions of the wheel of the quadriga, and a nearly perfect statue, which was almost certainly that of Mausolus, together with portions of two at least of the horses of the chariot. These enable us to restore that most important group with very tolerable certainty, and to ascertain that its height was somewhere about 13 or 14 feet.

Sixthly.—Portions of three different friezes were found, two of which appear to have been external; the third, from being less weather-worn, may have been situated under the pteron, or may have adorned the interior of the building.

Seventhly.—Fragments of some panels of sculpture, but where situated is not clear.

Eighthly.—In addition to these, fragments of a considerable number of statues, a little more than life-size, were discovered; and fragments, more or less perfect, of some 20 lions, principally of two dimensions, viz., either about 5 ft. 0 in. or 5 ft. 3 in. in length, and about the same in height; and one torso of what was either an Amazon or a young man on horseback in violent action.

Ninthly.—But perhaps the most important discovery of all, in so far as the restoration is concerned, was that the rock on which the building stood was excavated to a depth of 8 or 9 feet over an area measuring some 107 feet by 127. As the explorers were not aware of the value of these dimensions, they quote them loosely in round numbers; but they almost certainly were 105 by 126 Greek feet, or 106·31 English by 127·575, as will be explained hereafter.

3. *Exempla.*

By far the best corroborative example that has yet been brought to light is one discovered by Mr. Newton and his associates at Cnidus, and by them called the Lion Tomb.

1.—LION TOMB, CNIDUS.   (From Mr. Newton's work.)

Whether it is a Tomb at all, or whether the restoration can be depended upon, will not be known till the second part of Mr. Newton's text is published. The plates in his work fail, in this and every other instance, in giving the remotest idea of the remains *in situ*; and the architectural plates do not distinguish between what was found and what is restored. Still it must be near enough to the truth to be allowed to suggest what was the meaning of the "metæ cacumen," or the pedestal on which the sculpture was placed on the top of the Pyramid, which is the key to the whole mystery of the Mausoleum. It may also probably be quoted as suggesting the mode in which the Pyramid was placed on the order.

2. A Tomb is found at Dugga in Africa, which is singularly suggestive of the appearance of the Mausoleum, with only such difference as the very much smaller scale would necessitate.

2.—TOMB AT DUGGA.   (From a Drawing by Mr. Catherwood.)

3. A third, at Souma near Constantina, is published by Ravoisé in elevation, and in perspective by Mr. Falkener in his Museum of Classical Antiquities, No. 2, p. 172. This consists first of a solid podium or basement, with steps. Over this is a storey with a doorway or opening on each face, and above this a pteron of eight Doric columns, disposed three on each face, but without any cella or chamber, the space being too small to admit of any. There is, in this instance, no pyramid of steps on the top, but a small pediment on each face.

4. At page 174 of the same volume there is a still more suggestive design restored by Mr. Falkener from some remains he found at Denzili in Phrygia.

The base of this monument was entirely concealed by rubbish ; but above ground were found six square steles or piers, arranged three and three, with a figure sculptured in bas-relief on each face.   Above the entablature was a pyramid of steps supporting a couchant figure of a lion.

5. There is a well known Tomb at Mylassa, published by the Dilettante Society in their volume on 'Ionia ; ' which, though of late Roman times, is evidently copied from the Mausoleum.

3.—Tomb at Mylassa.

6. There are several other smaller examples, which, if they do not suggest much, are at least interesting, as showing how widely the fame of this building was extended, and how generally it was imitated, not only in Asia but in Africa.

7. There is also the Trophy Monument discovered by Sir Charles Fellows at Xanthus, which, though hardly bearing directly on the subject, is still sufficiently near it in design to suggest several peculiarities which, without its authority, we might hesitate to adopt.

4. *Rationes.* -

The last mode of investigation which has been mentioned as open to us, yields results which, though not so obvious at first sight, are quite as satisfactory as those obtained from any of the previously mentioned sources of information.

As will be explained in the sequel, we find that, by the application of the formula of simple ratios, we are enabled to fix the dimensions of almost every part of the Mausoleum with almost absolute certainty; and at the same time it is found that the Mausoleum is one of the most complete and interesting examples of a building designed wholly on a scheme of simple definite ratios. Thus the very science which assists materially in solving the problem, is at the same time illustrated and confirmed by the discoveries it aids in making.

The first attempt to explain the peculiarities of buildings by a scheme of definite ratios seems to be that expounded by Cæsar Cæsarini, in his edition of Vitruvius, published in 1521. In this work he shows by diagrams how a series of equilateral triangles explains all the dimensions and peculiarities of design in Milan Cathedral; and in this he probably was right, for, being a foreign work, it is very probable that the Italian architects, not understanding the true principles of the art, squeezed the design into this formal shape and so spoiled it. The success of this attempt of Cæsarini, however, has induced numberless other architects to apply the same principle to other Gothic Cathedrals, but without success in a single instance. Those which approach nearest to it are such buildings as Westminster Abbey,—a French church built in England; Cologne Cathedral, which is a French example in Germany; and in like manner all foreign examples approximate to definite proportions; but it may safely be asserted that no truly native example of Gothic art was so arranged.

It has, however, long been suspected that the Greeks proceeded on a totally different principle; but materials did not exist for a satisfactory elucidation of the question till Mr. Penrose published his exquisite survey of the Parthenon and other buildings at Athens made for the Society of Dilettanti, and Mr. Cockerell the result of his explorations at Bassæ and Egina. In the first-named work, its author pointed out with sufficient clearness some of the principal ratios of that celebrated building, which his survey enabled him to verify, and for others he supplied dimensions which for completeness and accuracy left nothing to be desired. With these new materials, Mr. Watkiss Lloyd undertook the investigation, and by a long and careful series of comparisons he has proved that the time-honoured doctrine of the Vitruvian school—that the lower diameter of a column was the modulus of every other part of a building—had no place in Greek art; on the contrary, that every part of a Greek building was proportioned to those parts in juxtaposition or analogy to it, in some such ratio as 3 to 4, 4 to 5, 5 to 6, and so on,—not by accident, but by careful study; and the whole design was evolved from a nexus of proportions as ingenious in themselves as they were harmonious in their result.

In the Parthenon, for instance, he found that the entire building is set

D

out with the minutest accuracy, by the application of a few ratios which involve no higher number than 16, and in no case have a higher difference between them than 5.

The greatest ingenuity and refinement were exercised in embracing the entire design in a network of proportional relations, in such a way that every division had a special dependence upon some other that was particularly contrasted or connected with it; and at the same time every member was implicated in more than one such comparison by what might seem happy accident, were it not that on trial it is proved how much study is required to effect such a result. At the same time, when the clue is once gained, it is easy to see how study was competent to effect it.

Among the proportional applications affecting the present subject, which may be considered axiomatic are these :—

The establishment of proportions of low numbers between—

1. The length and breadth of the basement, either upon its upper or lower step, or both.

2. The breadth of front and full height of·the building; in most cases, also, the length of flank and full height.

3. The length and breadth of any other conspicuous rectangle, such as in the present case would be the plans of the cella, of the pyramid, of the base or pedestal of the statue.

4. The division of the grand height of the structure into a pair of well-contrasted parts, having a ratio to each other of which the terms differ by unity, as 2 to 3, 3 to 4, &c. The further subdivision of these parts is effected again by definite proportions, and a favourite scheme here, as elsewhere, is for an intermediate section of a vertical line to have a simple proportion to the joint dimensions of sections above and below it, these upper and lower sections being then proportioned independently. Thus in the entablature of the Mausoleum the frieze is just half the joint height of architrave and cornice; that is, one-third of the height is given to the frieze.

5. The lower diameter of the Ionic column has usually a ratio to the upper diameter expressible in low numbers with a difference of unity. In the Mausoleum the ratio is 5 to 6, the same as at Priene. In the columns at Branchidæ, which were more than double the height, the difference is slighter, viz., 7 to 8.

6. The height of the column is usually, but by no means invariably, commensurable with the lower diameter, or at least semi-diameter, and the columns are spaced in one or other of the schemes that supply a symmetry with their height; that is to say, the height of the column will be found invariably to measure off a space laterally that coincides with centre and centre of columns, centre and margin, or margin and margin of the foot of the shaft or base. This

symmetry was of more importance than the commensurability of height by diameter.

7. In the architecture of temples, at least, the height either of the shaft or of the full column compares with the complementary height of the order, or of the front, in a ratio of which the terms differ by unity, and the larger term pertains to the columns. For example, the height of the Parthenon column is two parts out of three into which the full height of the order at the flank of the temple is divisible; the remaining part being divided between the entablature and the steps.*

Mr. Lloyd first publicly explained his theory of the system of proportions used in Greek architecture in a lecture he delivered at the Institute of British Architects in June, 1859, and he afterwards added an appendix to Mr. Cockerell's work on Egina and Bassæ, explaining specially the proportions of those temples; but the full development of his views, and particularly their relation to the Parthenon, which it appears surpassed all known works in refined and exact application of the system, still unfortunately remains in manuscript.

The more direct application of this theory to the design of the Mausoleum will be explained as we proceed, but in the meanwhile it may be asserted that without it many of the dimensions of this celebrated monument might for ever have remained matters of dispute. With its assistance there is scarcely one that may not be ascertained with almost absolute certainty.

Another and quite distinct set of ratios was discovered by Colonel Howard Vyse and his architect Mr. Perring, in their explorations of the Pyramids of Egypt. They found, for instance, in the Great Pyramid that the distance

	Cubits.
From the ground-line to the floor of the Queen's chamber was	40
From the floor of the Queen's to the floor of the King's chamber	40
From the floor of the King's chamber to the apex of the discharging roof . .	40
From that point to the apex of the pyramid, 40×4	160
Making up exactly	280

They also found that the length of the base line was to this dimension in the ratio of 8 to 5, making it 448 cubits or 767·424 feet English exactly. With these two dimensions all the other parts of so simple a figure follow as a matter of course.

The bearing of this also on the Mausoleum will be seen in the sequel, though a much more complicated system of ratios was of course necessary either to such a building or to even the very simplest Greek temples.

---

* These seven axioms or canons were furnished to me by Mr. Lloyd as leading results of his researches, after I had explained to him my theory of the mode in which the Mausoleum ought to be restored.

CHAPTER II.

Greek Measures.

THERE is one other point which must be carefully attended to in any attempt to restore the Mausoleum, which is the ratio between Greek and English measures. Those quoted by Pliny are in the former, of course; those obtained by the excavations are in the latter; and every result is vitiated and worthless without due attention to the difference.

The length of a Greek foot may be attained most directly by comparison with the Roman. From the researches of the best antiquaries as summed up by Niebuhr, the length of the Roman foot was ·972 English—a result confirmed by Mr. Penrose's careful independent investigation. Now, as it is known that the ratio between the Greek foot and the Roman was as 25 to 24, we arrive at the result of 101·25 English feet equal to 100 Greek.

Mr. Penrose obtained a slightly different result from his measurement of the upper step of the Parthenon. The front was known or assumed to be exactly 100 Greek feet; it gave 101·341, or about one inch in excess in 1200. As the flanks were to the front in the ratio of 4 to 9, this ought to have given 228·019. It was found to be 228·166, or nearly two inches in excess. But, on the other hand, it is admitted that the term Hecatompedon in Greek authors seems always to apply to the Naos and not to the step; and this, as measured by Mr. Penrose, including the transverse wall, gave 101·222, or a little under the other—the mean between the two being almost exactly identical with the measure derived from the Roman foot. In consequence of this the preference will be given throughout the following pages to the ratio of 101·25, or 101 ft. 3 in. English, as being equal to 100 Greek feet.

Turning from this to the measurement of the steps of the Pyramid, which, as mentioned above, is one of the most important elements for the restoration which have been brought to light by the recent excavations, we find their dimensions quoted throughout by Lieut. Smith, Mr. Pullan, and Mr. Newton as 1′ 9″, or 21 inches English for the wider, and 1′ 5″, or 17 English inches for the narrower step. The first thing that strikes one on considering this is, that it is a most wonderful coincidence that these dimensions should come out so exactly in English measures, without any fraction either way. On any moderate calculation of chances the odds are at least 100 to 1 against this being the case. The suspicion that there is an error somewhere is confirmed by observing that, though so very nearly in the ratio of 4 to 5, they are not exactly so; but if we try with the lower number we find 4 : 5 :: 17 : 21·25, or within the minutest fraction of 21 Greek inches.   If we adopt 17·01 English inches for the shorter, we have 21·2625, or exactly 21 Greek inches, for the latter.

It would be needless to attempt by measurement to attain such minute accuracy as this; as it must in fairness be stated that it is extremely difficult to ascertain minute differences in the present state of the remains.   Where two stones or steps are *in situ*, the one over the other, it is very easy to measure the distance from the face of the one to the face of the other; but when, as in this instance, we are dependent on the weather-marks or a position assumed from the details of other examples, we must be content with approximations, and without the guidance of some system of definite proportions can never be sure we are right.

The determination of this point was so essential that I have carefully measured all the angle and roofing stones I could get access to in the Museum, and find that, as nearly as can be ascertained, the dimension of 17 inches is correct; but the longer one is, it may be, ⁸⁄₁₀ths—it may be ⁹⁄₁₀ths—of an inch in excess.   Any one can verify this for himself; but I am so convinced of its correctness by my measurements, that I shall use the longer step as a dimension of 21 Greek, or 21·2625 English, inches.

Assuming this for the present, the next thing that suggests itself is, that 21 inches is the acknowledged length of the Babylonian cubit.   We know that after the captivity, the Jews added a handbreadth to their cubit, so as to make it up to this then fashionable measure; and as we know that Caria had been so long under the domination of the Persians, ruling from Babylon, there is no *à priori* improbability in this measure being current there.*

The well known tablets at Mylassa, given in Böckh, prove incontestably that Mausolus acknowledged himself a satrap of Artaxerxes as late as 355, or only two years before his death.   If it is contended that he afterwards emancipated himself from the Persian yoke—of which there is no proof—it is by no means clear that he did not commence his own tomb himself some time before his death.   At least it is nearly certain that no other man ever had a tomb of any great magnificence who did not in his lifetime take measures to secure its erection.

All this does not, it is true, prove that the Babylonian cubit was used in Caria; but it makes it so probable that it may have been that there will be nothing shocking in calling the length of the longer step by this name; and as this measure was the modulus of the whole building, and occurs over and over again, it will be convenient, and avoid circumlocution, if—of course,

---

* If we can depend on Mr. Perring's determination, the Egyptian cubit used in fixing the dimensions of the Great Pyramid was more than half an inch shorter than the Babylonian or Halicarnassean cubit used for that purpose in the Mausoleum.   As far as can be ascertained, the Egyptian equalled 1·713 foot English, while the other was 1·771; the difference being fifty-eight thousandths of a foot, or nearly two-thirds of an inch

without prejudging the fact—we call the measure of 21 Greek inches as equal to 1 Babylonian or Halicarnassean cubit. If it could be proved that such a measure was never known in Caria, this would not in the least affect the result. All that is wanted here is a name which shall express a measure of 21 Greek inches. If any other can be suggested it will answer equally well. But it seems necessary that some definite term should be used in the sequel; and, till some other is found, I may perhaps be allowed to employ this.

Cymatium.

Next in importance to the steps of the Pyramid, for the purposes of restoration, are the fragments of the Cymatium which were discovered in the excavations. Of these some six or seven were found, and on each was either a Lion's head covering the joint, or the mark of a Lion's head on the further edge of the stone next the joint.

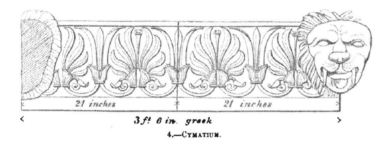

4.—Cymatium.

Each of these pieces was, like the steps of the Pyramid, 21 inches, or 1 cubit, in length;* and, according to the evidence we now have, the Lions' heads were consequently spaced 2 cubits, or 3 feet 6 inches, from the centre of one to the centre of another.

The interest of this measurement lies in the certainty that the inter-columniation was somehow commensurate with it. The usual arrangement in Greek architecture would have been that there should be one Lion's head over the centre of each column, and one half-way between. This certainly was not the arrangement here, as the columns, which are 3 ft. 6 in. Greek, or exactly 2 cubits in width, in their lower diameter, would then have been only one diameter apart.

It has been suggested that, as the Lions' heads are so unusually close, the pillars may have been so arranged that one column had a Lion's head over its

---

* They are so much broken and so carelessly put together in the Museum, that, if we had no other evidence, it might be contended they were either 20½ inches or 21½; but on a fair average measurement there can be no doubt that 21 Greek inches is the correct modulus.

centre, and those on each side stood between two Lions' heads—thus making the intercolumniation 8 ft. 9 in.   The first objection that occurs to this view is, that it is unknown in any other examples ; that it is contrary to the general principles of the art, and introduces an unnecessary complication ; and is, therefore, unlikely.   But the great objection is, that it cannot be made to fit in with any arrangement of the Pyramid steps.   Let it be assumed, for instance, that the thirty-six columns of the Pteron were so arranged as to give an uneven number each way, so as to have eleven intercolumniations on one side by seven on the other ; this would give a dimension of 96 feet 3 inches by 61 feet 3 inches from centre to centre of the angle columns, to which it would be impossible to fit the Pyramid, assuming, from the evidence of the steps, that its sides were in ratio 4 to 5, or nearly so at all events.   If, on the contrary, it is assumed that there were 10 intercolumniations by 8, this would give a dimension of 87·6 by 70 ; and adding 2 ft. 9 in. each way, which we shall presently see was the projection of the first step of the Pyramid beyond the centre of the angle column, we should have for its base 93 feet by 75 feet 6 inches, within which it is impossible to compress it, unless we adopt a tall pyramid, as was done by Mr. Cockerell and Mr. Falkener before the discovery of the pyramid steps, or unless we admit of a curvi-linear-formed pyramid, as was suggested by myself.   With the evidence that is now before us, neither of these suggestions seems to be for one moment tenable ; and as we cannot, with this intercolumniation, stretch the dimensions of the Pteron beyond what is stated above, it must be abandoned.

Advancing 1 cubit beyond this, we come to 6 cubits, or 10 feet 6 inches Greek, as the distance from the centre of one column to the centre of the next ;* and the Lions' heads then range symmetrically, one over each pillar, and two between each pair.

At first sight there seems to be no objection to the assumption that one plain piece of the Cymatium may have been inserted between each of the pieces to which were attached the Lions' heads, or the impress of them.   It is true none were found ; but as there could be only one plain piece in three, and as only six or seven fragments were found altogether, the chances against this theory are not sufficient to cause its rejection.   The real difficulty is, that a Lion's head exists on a stone 1 cubit from the angle; and, unless the architects adopted a different arrangement at the angles from what they did in the centre, which is, to say the least of it, extremely improbable, it cannot be made to fit with the arrangement.   If one plain piece had been found, it would have fixed the distance between centre and centre of column at 10 ft. 6 in. absolutely.   As none, however, were found, or at least brought home, we must look for our proofs elsewhere.

----

* It is hardly worth while to allude to Mr. Pullan's dimension of 10 English feet from centre to centre. It agrees with no fact and no theory.

The first of these is a very satisfactory one, on the principle of definite proportions above explained. As we have just found that six pyramid steps, or 6 cubits, are equal to one intercolumniation, so six intercolumniations, or 36 cubits, is exactly 63 Greek feet—the "sexagenos ternos pedes," which Pliny ascribes to the cella or tomb; it is further proved that this was not accidental, by our finding that twice the length of the cella, or 126 Greek feet, or 72 cubits, is, or ought to be, the total length of the building, measured on its lowest step. This, as before mentioned, Mr. Newton quotes, in round numbers, as 127 feet English; but as neither he nor any of those with him had any idea that any peculiar value was attached to this dimension, they measured carelessly and quoted loosely. My own conviction is, that it certainly was 127 ft. 6¾ in. English, which would be the exact equivalent of 126 Greek feet. At all events, I feel perfectly certain that the best mode of ascertaining the exact length of the pyramid step would be to divide this dimension, whatever it is, by 72.

Pteron.

Returning to the Pteron: if the columns were ranged in a single row—and no other arrangement seems possible with the evidence now before us—there must have been eleven columns on the longer faces and nine at the ends, counting the angle columns twice, and consequently a column in the centre of each face. This, at least, is the resultant of every conceivable hypothesis that I have been able to try. No other will, even in a remote degree, suit the admitted forms and dimensions of the pyramid: it is that adopted by Lieutenant Smith and Mr. Pullan; and, according to the evidence before us, seems the only one admissible.

Adopting it for the present, the first difficulty that arises is that 10 intercolumniations at 10 ft. 6 in. give 105 feet; to which if we add as before 5 ft. 6 in., or twice 2 ft. 9 in., for the projection of the first step of the pyramid beyond the centres of the columns, we have 110 ft. 6 in., a dimension to which it is almost impossible to extend the pyramid; and, what is worse, with a cella only 63 feet in its longest dimension, it leaves 21 feet at either end, from the centre of the columns to the wall, a space which it is almost impossible could be roofed by any of the expedients known to the Greeks; and the flanks are almost equally intractable. It was this that rendered Lieutenant Smith's restoration so unacceptable. He boldly and honestly faced the difficulty, and so far he did good service, and deserves all praise. Mr. Pullan's expedient of cutting 6 inches off each intercolumniation is not so creditable, nor is the result much more satisfactory.

After trying several others, the solution appears to me to lie in the hypothesis that the angle columns were coupled,—or, in other words, half an intercolumniation (5 feet 3 inches) apart from centre to centre.

Should it be asked if there are any other examples of this arrangement, the answer must probably be that there are not ; but there is also no other building known with a pyramidal roof, or which, from its design, would so much require strengthening at the angles.   The distance between the columns and the front must necessarily be so great,—the height at which they are placed is so considerable,—and the form of the roof so exceptional, that I feel quite certain any architect will admit that this grouping together of the angle columns is æsthetically an improvement.*

Although this arrangement may not be found in any Ionic edifice, it is a well-known fact that in every Doric Temple the three columns at the angles are spaced nearer to each other than those intermediate between them, either in the flanks or front.   The usual theory is that this was done to accommodate the exigencies of the triglyphs.   It may be so, but the Greeks were too ingenious a people to allow any such difficulty to control their designs if they had not thought it an improvement to strengthen the angles of their buildings.   We may also again refer to the Lion Tomb at Cnidus (Woodcut, No. 1), where the angle intercolumniations are less than the centre ones, for no conceivable reason but to give apparent strength to that part.

The proof, however, must depend on how it fits with the other parts.

Taking first the flanks, we have 8 whole and 2 half intercolumniations, equal to 94 feet 6 inches Greek, or 48 cubits, or just once and a half the length of the cella ; which is so far satisfactory.   At the back of the gutter behind the cymatium there is a weather mark which certainly indicates the position of the first step of the pyramid, and, according to Mr. Pullan's restoration of the order, this mark is 2 ft. 8½ in. beyond the centre of the columns.   As there are a great many doubtful elements in this restoration, and as, from the fragmentary nature of the evidence, it is impossible to be certain within half an inch or even an inch either way, let us, for the nonce, assume this dimension to be 2 ft. 9 in.   Twice this for the projection either way, or 5 ft. 6 in., added to 94 ft. 6 in., gives exactly 100 Greek feet for the dimension of the lowest step of the pyramid.   So far nothing could be more satisfactory ; but, if it is of any value, the opposite side ought to be 80 feet,—or in the ratio of 5 to 4.

On this side we have 6 whole and 2 half intercolumniations, or 73 ft. 6 in.,—to which adding, as before, 5 ft. 6 in. for the projection of the step, we obtain 79 feet !   If this is really so, there is an end of this theory of restoration on a system of definite proportions ; and so for a long time I thought, and was inclined to give up the whole in despair.   The solution, however, does not seem difficult when once it is explained.   It probably is this : the steps of the Pyramid being in the ratio of

---

* As I first restored the building I placed a square anta in the angles, with pilasters on each face, as are found in the angles of the Erectheium at Athens.   I had overlooked the fact that a capital was found with an angular volute, which settles the question ; but I still think that architecturally the square pier arrangement would have been the best.

E

4 to 5, or as 16·8 in. to 21 inches Greek, the cymatium gutter must be in the same ratio, or the angle would not be in the same line with the angles of the steps or of the pedestals, or whatever was used to finish the roof.   In Mr. Newton's text this dimension is called 1 ft. 10 in. throughout; according to Mr. Day's lithographer it is 1'·88, which does not represent 1 ft. 10 in. by any system of decimal notation I am acquainted with.   According to Mr. Pullan's drawing it scales 2 feet.*   From internal evidence, I fancy the latter is the true dimension.   Assuming it to be so, and that it is the narrowest of the two gutters, the other was of course as 4 is to 5, or as 2 feet to 2 feet 6 inches, which gives us the exact dimensions we are seeking, or 6 inches each way.   This I feel convinced is the true explanation, but the difficulty is that, if it is so, there must be some error in Mr. Pullan's restoration of the order.   If we assume that we have got the wider gutter, the other would be 19·2 in., which would be easily adjusted to the order, but would give only 4·8 in. each way, or 1⅖ in. less than is wanted.   It is so unlikely that the Greeks would have allowed their system to break down for so small a quantity as one inch and one-fifth in 40 feet, that we may feel certain—if this difficulty exists at all—that it is only our ignorance that prevents our perceiving how it was adjusted.   If it should prove that the cymatium we have got is the larger one, and that consequently this difference does exist, the solution will probably be found in the fact of the existence of two roof stones, with the abnormal dimensions quoted by Mr. Pullan as 10½ inches and 9 respectively. It may be they were 9" and 10"·2, which would give the quantity wanted. But, whatever their exact dimensions, it is probable that they were the lowest steps of the pyramid; and, if the discrepancy above alluded to did exist, they may have been used as the means of adjusting it.   Be all this as it may, I feel convinced that whenever the fragments can be carefully re-examined, it will be found that the exact dimension we are seeking was 80 Greek feet.†

        There is another test to which this arrangement of the columns must be

---

* Nothing can be more unsatisfactory than the system of scales used in Mr. Newton's work. They are in feet and decimals of a foot; a mode of notation very rarely used for any purpose, and never, so far as I know, adopted by any architect in his professional practice. The consequence is that such scales are not to be purchased ; and if ordered there is the greatest possible difficulty in getting them made. The inconvenience is aggravated in this case by the slovenly practice of not putting scales to the plates: all the information the engraver condescends to is " Scale 1 ÷ 30," or " 1 ÷ 10," &c., as the case may be. The consequence is that not one person in a hundred understands to what scale the drawings are made, and not one in a thousand will take the trouble to construct the scales which are indispensably necessary to enable him to study the plates.

    † As a proper punishment for the introduction of

so troublesome a novelty as these decimal scales, either the draftsman or lithographer has separated by a dot all the first figures of the decimals in the plate of the restored order (Plate xxii.). A dimension, therefore, which reads 2·96 or two feet eleven inches and a fraction in plate xxi., reads 2 ft. 9·6, or two feet nine inches and a fraction, in plate xxii. The lower diameter, which scales three feet six inches and one-third, reads three feet five inches and one-third, and so on. In fact, nine-tenths of the dimensions are absolutely wrong. The remaining tenth are right by accident; but most of these are so, simply because the lithographer has been too lazy or too inaccurate to put any sign by which they can be read. All this not only increases tenfold the labour of consulting the plates, but renders it doubtful whether frequently it is not a mere fighting with shadows to contest any theory on such documents.

submitted before it can be accepted, which is, the manner in which it can be made to accord with the width of the cella.

The first hypothesis that one naturally adopts is that the peristyle should be one intercolumniation in width, in other words that the distance between the centres of the columns and the walls of the cella should be 10 feet 6 inches. Assuming this, or deducting 21 Greek feet from the extreme width we have just found above of 73 feet 6 inches, it leaves 52 feet 6 inches for the width, which is a very reasonable explanation of Pliny's expression, " brevius a frontibus." It is also satisfactory, as it is in the proportion of 5 to 6, with 63 feet, which is Pliny's dimension, for the length of the cella. But the " instantia crucis" must be that it should turn out—like the longer sides—just one half the lower step, or rock-cut excavation. What this is, is not so easily ascertained. In his letter to Lord Stratford de Redcliffe, of 3rd April, 1857, Mr. Newton calls it 110 feet; in the text (p. 95) it is called 108 ; while Lieut. Smith, who probably made the measurement, calls it 107 (Parl. Papers, p. 20). The latter, therefore, we may assume is the most correct. If the above hypothesis is correct, it ought to have been 106·31 English or 105 Greek feet, which most probably was really the dimension found ; but as it did not appear to the excavators that anything depended upon it, they measured it, as before, carelessly and recorded it more so.

In the meanwhile, therefore, we may assume that the width of the cella was 52 feet 6 inches, or 30 Babylonian cubits. The width of the lower step on the east and west fronts was 105 Greek feet, or 60 cubits exactly.

Of course this is exactly in the proportion of 5 to 6 with the longer step, which, as we found above, was 72 cubits or 126 Greek feet; and this, as we shall presently see, was the exact height of the building without the quadriga, the total height being 80 cubits or 140 Greek feet.

Pyramid.

Having now obtained a reasonable proportion for the lower step of the Pyramid, 100 by 80 Greek feet, the remaining dimensions are easily ascertained.

Mr. Pullan, using the nearly correct measure of 17 English inches for the shorter step, obtained 32 feet 6 inches English for the spread of the pyramid in one direction. It need hardly be remarked that when there were 24 joints, and each stone sloped slightly backwards instead of having its face perpendicular to its bed, it is impossible now to attain any minute accuracy in this dimension ; but 32·5 ft. English is so nearly 32 Greek feet (it ought to have been 32'·4) that we may fairly assume that that was the dimension intended, the difference being very slightly in excess of one inch.

In the other direction Mr. Pullan obtained 39' 11½" English ; but as it is impossible, for the reasons just stated, to ascertain to half an inch what this dimension really was, we may assume this to be 40 English feet; and as Mr. Pullan used the erroneous measurement of 21 English instead of 21 Greek inches, we at once obtain 40 Greek feet for the spread in the longer direction, or again in the ratio of 4 to 5.

This leaves a platform on the summit of 20 Greek feet by 16, on which to erect the pedestal or meta, which is to support the quadriga. The question is,—is it sufficient?

According to Mr. Pullan's drawings (Plates XVIII. and XX.), the group measures 15 feet English in length by 13′ 6″ across, and 12′ 6″ from the extreme hoof on one side to that on the other. This, however, hardly accords with the facts stated in the text.* It is stated at page 162, that the horses measure each 3 feet 6 inches across the chest, which alone makes 14 feet, supposing them to stand with their shoulders touching each other. Between the two central horses was the pole, which may have measured 9 inches, and as it could hardly be supported otherwise, if of marble, probably touched the shoulder of the horse on either side; and, allowing the same distance between the two outer horses, we get 16′ 3″ English, or, as near as may be, 16 Greek feet for the extreme width of the group. This, however, is probably overstating the matter; 3′ 6″ seems an extreme measurement, in so far as I can ascertain. There is no proof that they were all so, and 6 inches is sufficient for the width between the outer horses. This dimension may therefore be stated as between 15 and 16 Greek feet. The width of the plinth would be less than either, for a horse stands considerably within his extreme breadth, and I need hardly say that anywhere, but more especially at such a height as this, a sculptor would bring the hoof as near the edge of the plinth as possible. In the Museum, there is one hoof of one of the chariot-horses placed within 2 inches of the edge of the stone on which it stands; but this does not seem to have been an outside stone; though the same dimensions would be ample if it were. There is no difficulty, therefore, in this dimension; the plinth probably may have been 15 Greek feet, which would allow 6 inches either way for the projection of the step.

In the other direction, the length seems somewhat excessive. From the front to the rear hoofs of the horses, there may have been about 10 feet; the chariot-wheel is said to have been 7 ft. 7 in., and the length of the pedestal required would consequently be about that dimension, or 17 ft. 7 in. English. It is probable, however, that the figure of the Goddess stood outside the chariot behind, and this would easily fill up the whole. But at the same time, is it quite clear that the chariot stood as assumed above, or parallel to the longer axis of the building? The principal approach, we know from Vitruvius, was from the south. The pyramid was steepest on that side, and there would be

---

* In a note in p. 162 it is stated that "the wheel is made somewhat smaller than its true scale, as if drawn in strict elevation it would convey a false impression of the effect of the original group." On what theory, it is difficult to understand; but there is nothing to intimate that the figures or horses are not to the scale 1 ÷ 10, which is marked on the plate. Either, however, the text or the drawing is wrong; unless both are so, which seems probable.

infinitely more symmetry in the principal group facing in that direction than in the other.   In that case, we must assume that the horses that have been recovered are the central ones, and in comparative repose.   The outer ones would be in more violent action, and spread wider.   This is, perhaps, more a sculptor's question than an architect's : but my own feeling is strongly in favour of the last hypothesis.   It seems more in accordance with what we know of Greek art, and artistically I cannot help fancying it would look better from every point of view than if the chariot group was placed, as in Plate II., facing towards the longer sides of the building.*

Before leaving the pyramid, there is one little matter which requires adjustment.   Two steps were found differing from the others, and measuring 9 inches and 10½ inches in width respectively.   Mr. Pullan places these at the top of the pyramid, where it appears they must have made a very unpleasing break in the uniformity of the lines.   I fancy they were the lowest steps of all.

As will be observed from the diagram (Woodcut No. 5) the lowest step of

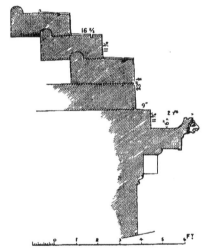

5.—SECTION OF CYMATIUM AND OF BASE OF PYRAMID.

the pyramid is buried to half its height in the gutter behind the cymatium ; and with that projecting 2 feet beyond, it could not be seen anywhere within

---

* In Plate II. of this work the chariot group is represented as facing transversely, in the Frontispiece and Plate III. as facing longitudinally to the building. It may be as well to mention here that I have introduced several such discrepancies into the plates, which are neither oversights nor errors. This is one; another is that, in Plate II., the lions at the angles of the pyramid are omitted, but inserted in the other three plates : a cymatium has been introduced as crowning the order of the base in one plate, and another mould-ing substituted in the others. The Monte Cavallo groups have been introduced in Plates I. and III. and omitted elsewhere. The object of these alterations is that, as these are mere suggestions, they are offered as such in order that the reader may exercise his own judgment regarding them. The dimensions, and all those parts which are certain, are repeated throughout; but, unless some further discoveries are made, there must always be some details which must be left to the taste or the knowledge of the restorer.

400 feet of the building,—practically not at all.   At the same time I am inclined to believe that the lowest visible step was at least twice as high as the others.   The authority for this is, of course, the Lion Tomb (Woodcut No. 1); but I think every architect will agree that a pyramid fading away behind a cymatium, without any marking line, would be most unpleasing architecturally; and especially when the pyramid slopes upwards at so low an angle, and is placed so high, the arrangement seems especially wanted.   Assuming this, the 9-inch step is just what is required to bring the taller step perpendicular over the frieze, and preventing the cymatium at the same time appearing to have too great a projection at such points as it could be seen from.   Mr. Pullan makes the whole height of the twenty-four steps equal to 25 feet English.   If this were added it would be 26, or about 25 feet 9 inches Greek; leaving thus 11 feet 9 inches for the height of the meta or pedestal of the quadriga.

In so far as any accordance with Pliny's dimensions is concerned, the height of the pyramid steps is not of the smallest consequence.   Whatever is added to the pyramid must be taken from the meta; whatever is taken from the meta, which there is nothing to govern, must be added to the pyramid.   What its height really was, can only be ascertained when some system of definite proportions for the vertical heights of the building shall have been satisfactorily settled, which, as will be explained farther on, is rather difficult to establish absolutely, though easy to fix within certain tolerably narrow limits.

Vertical Heights.

With regard to the vertical heights, there is absolutely no difficulty in making them agree with those found in Pliny.   The pyramid,—" in metæ cacumen se contrahens,"—was 25 Greek cubits, or 37 ft. 6 in.   The order was the same in height exactly, and if we choose to assume that the expression " pyramis altitudine inferiorem æquavit" referred to the pteron as the " lower part," it comes out correctly.   If we add to the pyramid the quadriga, estimating that at 13' 9", we have 51' 3", and taking the same quantity for the basement, we have

		Greek Ft.	In.
For the pyramid and quadriga		51	3
For the basement		51	3
For the pteron 25 cubits		37	6
		140	0

or exactly the dimensions found in Pliny.

All this is so clear and so satisfactory, that there the matter might rest. There is no real necessity to look further, were it not that one or two peculiarities come out in the investigation which seem worthy of being noted.

In restoring the basement, after making its entablature of such proportions as seemed to me most appropriate, I was surprised to find, on applying a scale, that I had obtained exactly 37 ft. 6 in. for the height from the ground line to the soffit over the piers. Though I have tried several other dimensions since, this seems so appropriate that, as very little depends on it, we may allow it to stand.

Assuming this, therefore, we find the height dividing itself into three portions, each of which was 37 ft. 6 in., and two which seem to be 13 ft. 9 in. each. But if this were so, we come to the difficulty that there is no very obvious rule of proportion between these parts, which there certainly ought to be. Even if we add the two smaller ones together we obtain 27 ft. 6 in., which, though nearly, is not quite in the ratio of 3 to 4 to the larger dimension of 37 ft. 6 in. If we add to the first 9 inches we get the exact ratio we require; but by this process increase the height of the building by that dimension, which is impossible.

The explanation of the difficulty may perhaps be found in the fact that the order overlaps the pyramid nearly to that extent, as is seen in the diagram (Woodcut No. 5.) It is by no means improbable that the architects made the pyramid 37 ft. 6 in. from the bottom of the bottom step,—as they naturally would,—and measured the order to the top of the cymatium; and consequently these two dimensions added together did not make 75 feet, but 74 ft. 3 in., or something very near to it.

There is a curious confirmation of this in another dimension which must not be overlooked. At page 24 we found the extreme length of the building to be 126 feet, or 72 Babylonian cubits. This ought to be the height; and so it is, to an inch, if we allow the quadriga to have measured 14 Greek feet. Mr. Newton, it is true, makes it only 13 ft. 3 in. English, but it was necessary for his theory of restoration to keep it as low as possible; and, though it may have been only that height, there are no data to prevent its being higher, nor indeed to fix its dimensions within the margin of a foot. Considering the height at which it was seen, there is everything to confirm the latter dimension, which has besides the merit of being exactly one-tenth of the total height of the building.

From these data we obtain for the probable height of the different parts of the building the following :—

	Ft.	In.
Height of basement to soffit	37	6
Entablature of ditto	14	0
Pteron, to top of cymatium	37	6
Pyramid	37	6
Quadriga	14	0
	140	6
Deduct for overlap		6* (9?)
	140	0

* There is a discrepancy of three inches in this dimension, which must be apportioned somewhere. I fancy it is to be found in the cymatium gutter, but this could only be ascertained from a thorough re-examination of the fragments themselves.

or exactly 80 Babylonian cubits, which is probably the dimension Hyginus copied out, though either he or some bungling copier wrote " feet " for " cubits," just as the lithographers have altered all Mr. Pullan's decimals of a foot into inches, because they did not understand the unusual measures which were being made use of.

There is still another mode in which this question may be looked at. It appears so strange that the architects should have used one modulus for the plan and another for the height, that I cannot help suspecting that in Satyrus's work the dimensions were called 21 Babylonian or 25 Greek cubits, or some such expression. The difference is not great (9 inches), and it seems so curious that Greek cubits should have been introduced at all that we cannot help trying to find out how it was.

In the previous investigation it appeared that the only two vertical dimensions obtained beyond those quoted by Pliny which were absolutely certain were 126 feet or 72 cubits for the height of the building, and 8 cubits or 14 feet for the quadriga. Now, if we assume thrice 21 cubits for the height, we have 63 cubits, and this with 8 cubits for the quadriga, and 9 for the entablature of the basement, making together 17 cubits, complete the 80 we are looking for. In other words, we return to the identical ratios from which we started, of 17″ and 21″, if these figures represented in inches the dimensions of the steps, as they are always assumed to be by Messrs. Newton, and Pullan, and Smith. If it were so, nothing could be more satisfactory; but, to make the ratio perfect, the last dimension, instead of 9 cubits, ought to be 8·8; so that we should get a total of 4 inches too short, instead of being in excess, as it was by the last calculation.

It would, of course, be easy to apportion this as one inch to each of the four parts; but that is inadmissible in a building planned with such exactitude as this, and I therefore merely state it in order to draw to it the attention of some one cleverer at ratios than I am, confessing that I am beaten, though only by an inch.

Personally I feel inclined to believe that the architects were content to use the figures of their plan in determining their heights, and made them 8, 9, 21, 63, 72, 80 cubits, &c., and to obtain this were content with the imperfect ratio of 17 to 21. By this process it will be observed that they obtained the ratio that the first figure should be $\frac{1}{8}$ and $\frac{1}{10}$ of the two last respectively, and the second figure $\frac{1}{7}$ and $\frac{1}{8}$ of 63 and 72 respectively; and there may be other ratios which I have failed to detect. The real difficulty is, that this involves abandoning to a certain extent Pliny's figures, which at present I do not feel inclined to agree to. All this, however, is mere idle speculation, in no way affecting the scheme of restoration, though amusing as a problem in Greek art.

Architectural Ordinance.

Having now obtained all the dimensions of the building, except the 411 feet as the " totus circuitus " mentioned by Pliny, to which we shall come presently, the next point is to explain the architectural peculiarities of the structure.

Unfortunately neither Pliny nor any other ancient author gives us the smallest hint as to how the interior of the building was arranged, and were it not for Guichard's narrative we should have nothing but the analogy of other buildings to guide us. His account of the remains, and of the discovery of the chamber in the basement, is so clear, so circumstantial, and in every respect so probable, that there does not seem any reason to doubt that it was substantially correct, and no restoration can be accepted which does not admit of and explain its details.

Although it is true no such catastrophe is expressly mentioned by any author, the position in which the horses of the quadriga were found renders it almost certain that the upper part of the building had been shaken down by an earthquake prior to the year 1402.

Had the building been perfect, it is hardly probable that even such barbarians as the Knights of St. John would have knocked it down; but, be this as it may, in 1522 it seems that the basement was covered up by the *débris* of the upper part and other rubbish, probably also by the sand and dust entangled in the heap. In consequence of this it was not till after a considerable quantity of the ruins had been removed that the Knights " saw an opening such as would lead into a cellar, and, taking a candle, let themselves down into the interior, where they found a beautiful large square hall, ornamented all round with columns of marble, with their bases, capitals, friezes, cornices, engraved and sculptured in half-relief. The space between the columns was lined with slabs and bands or fillets of marble of different colours, ornamented with mouldings and sculptures in harmony with the rest of the work, and inserted in the white ground of the wall, where battle-scenes were represented sculptured in half-relief." *

It is not quite clear whether the hole the Knights found was in the roof of the apartment or in its side, at some height above the floor. I strongly suspect the latter, but of this more hereafter. From the description it is quite clear that this hall was not the cella surrounded by the pteron as described by Pliny; for on any theory of restoration the floor of that must have been 50 feet from the ground, and it could consequently neither have been buried nor could the Knights have descended into it. It must have been in the basement, and if so must have been lighted. For it need hardly be stated that the Greeks

---

* See page 11 ante.

F

would never have applied such an amount of ornamentation to a hall where it could not have been perfectly seen.* It could not have been lighted by windows in the ordinary sense of the term, as its walls could not be less than 21 feet thick, but there seems no difficulty in introducing any amount of light required by the mode suggested in the accompanying plan and sections.† As shown there, there are four openings on each side, 17 feet high by about 6½ wide, opening into a corridor 8 ft. 6 in. in width, which was separated from the outer air by piers 4 feet in width. It was, in fact, a *peristele* under a *peristyle*. As these words exactly express the difference between the two corridors, they will be so used in future—peristele (from περι and στήλη, a stele) being used for the lower, and peristyle (from στυλος, a column) for the colonnade which it supported. If more light was wanted, it could be introduced to any desired extent at the end opposite the door, but the eight openings shown in the plan are, it is conceived, more than sufficient. By this arrangement, too, the light is introduced in the most pleasing manner. The direct rays of the sun could never penetrate the sepulchral chamber, but a diffused high light was introduced sufficient to show all its beauties without disturbing its repose.

The existence of some such arrangement as this appears indispensable in order to understand the passage in Martial :—

> " Aere nec vacuo pendentia Mausolea
> Laudibus immodicis Cares ad astra ferant."

It is absurd to suggest that this might refer to some little structural difficulties about a roof, as no roof was ever less seen than that of this building. Besides, a roof is not a mausoleum ; but the upper chamber here was so called, according to Pliny ; and the fact, therefore, of people being able to walk round the building and see the town on one side, or the shipping and the sea on the other, through it, *under its floor*, may well have led the Halicarnassians to boast that their great tomb was supported in the air. This would in those days be even more striking than at present, inasmuch as there was not, so far as we now know, a single two-storied temple or tomb of any importance then existing.

With regard to the dimensions of the chamber, we found above that the upper one was, externally, 63 Greek feet by 52 ft. 6 in., or in the ratio of 5 to 6 ; and if we deduct half an intercolumniation, or 3 cubits, for the thickness of the walls, we attain 52 ft. 6 in. by 42 feet for the internal dimensions ; which is probable,

---

* The mode of lighting Greek temples and Greek buildings generally has never fully been investigated by architects. I read a short paper on the subject at the Royal Institute of British Architects on the 18th of November last ; and though that is an amplification of my remarks in the True Principles of Beauty in Art some fourteen years ago, it is far from exhausting the subject. But it is enough to prove that the mode of introducing light was as perfect and as beautiful as every other part and every other contrivance of Greek architecture.

† Plates I. II. and III.

inasmuch as it comes out in the ratio of 4 to 5, and is besides a very probable constructive dimension with reference to the mass of the roof, which was almost wholly supported on these walls. The dimensions of the lower apartment were in all probability identical with those of the upper room. With regard to the mode in which the upper chamber was lighted there can be no difficulty. Four windows are introduced in each side, similar in design to those of the Temple of Minerva Polias at Athens. Less would do ; but as it is easier to subdue than to increase the light, it probably was thus.

Both these rooms probably had flat marble roofs. The lower one almost certainly had ; and if so, there must have been columns in the centre, as it would have been impossible to throw a marble beam across an apartment 42 feet in width. These pillars would not only add very considerably to their beauty architecturally, but may also to a certain extent have been useful in steadying the external roof ; not indeed that this was required, for, whether it was constructed on the principle of a horizontal or of a radiating arch, the abutment and walls are quite sufficient for its support. At this day we should certainly employ a radiating construction ; the architects may have preferred the horizontal arch in those days.

For the upper chamber I have suggested a niche at the upper end, opposite the door, where an altar probably was placed ; and on either side I fancy there would be sarcophagi, not to contain bodies, but to suggest rites. Such at least is the usual arrangement in all the great tombs I know.

If this apartment was as magnificent as I suppose it to have been, there was, of course, easy access to it, which may without difficulty be attained by the means suggested on the plan (Plate I.). According to this scheme, as a visitor entered the building between the two great piers in the eastern front, he might either ascend by the stairs on his right hand or his left to the peristele ; or by the great door in front of him, beyond the stairs, he might enter the lower chamber. From the peristele a second flight of equal extent led to a landing from which a third flight gave access to the peristyle in such a manner as to leave the entrance to the chamber as unencumbered as possible, as probably an altar was placed there.

It will be observed that each of the flights of stairs was perfectly lighted, the lower and upper being open above, and the intermediate flight open from the side. Their existence here will also explain why the intercolumniation was deeper by one-half in front of the cella than in the flanks. But for this difference, the stairs, instead of being 5 ft. 6 in. in width, could barely have been 2 feet wide.

The only other apartment for which it is necessary to find a place in the building is the tomb itself. This fortunately is no difficulty, as the excavated stairs at the west end of the building, and the big stone which was found there, certainly indicate its whereabouts, even if they do not actually fix the spot.

Besides this, the expressions used by Guichard in themselves almost suffice—
" It was situated beyond a low doorway, after the manner of an antechamber."
This cannot, of course, apply to a vault under the hall first discovered by the
Knights, but describes accurately such a chamber as the wider intercolumniations
at the further end would fully admit of, while the fact of the stairs being exca-
vated * gives the requisite height without interfering with the peristele above.

In the plan and sections I have suggested stairs leading down to it; and
even if it is insisted that the Tomb of Mausolus, on the right, was walled up,†
and the stones let down immediately after the interment, it does not follow that
the Tomb of Artemisia, which probably was on the left, may not have been
accessible long afterwards; and there may have been other vaults beneath to
which it was desirable to give means of access.

There may also have been recesses for sarcophagi or urns in the thickness
of the walls on either side of the principal chamber, as represented in the plan;
but these are details it is hardly worth while entering into at present.   There
is no authority for them, so every one may supply or reject them as suits his
own fancy.

Lacunaria.

One further merit of the restoration just described is, that it entirely gets
over the difficulty of the Lacunaria of the peristyle, which rendered Lieut.
Smith's proposal so inadmissible.   With the arrangement of the columns here
suggested, and the dimensions obtained for the cella, the greatest width to be
spanned in front and rear is only 14 Greek feet—2 feet 8 inches less than Mr.
Pullan makes it.   Although it is just such an increase as this that makes the
difficulty in most cases, neither of these dimensions ought to be considered
insuperable, inasmuch as in the Propylæa at Athens a marble roof is thrown
over a clear space of 18 feet 6 inches English; and though it may be suggested
that the roof over these Lacunaria was lighter, that does not alter the case.
No part of the external roof of the Mausoleum rested on these beams, and they
therefore were not affected by its weight.

It is not necessary here to go into a detailed examination of the one
lacunar stone that has been found and brought home.   Mr. Pullan thinks it
requires a 10 feet intercolumniation, Mr. Cockerell one of 8 feet 9 inches; but
neither know, or can know, what part of the building it comes from, or whether
it was placed lengthways or transversely to the beams.   Under these circum-

---

* These stairs, indicated by dotted lines in the plan
(Plate I.) being on one side, clearly indicate that the
sepulchre was not symmetrically placed to occupy the
centre of the building. Curiously enough, the Tomb at
Mylassa (Woodcut No. 3) has a doorway placed unsym-
metrically, for no reason that can be guessed, unless it
were in imitation of its celebrated prototype. What
also is curious is that at Mylassa a pillar stands directly

over the centre of the doorway leading into the principal chamber of the tomb, exactly as occurs at
Halicarnassus, and that chamber has a flat stone-roof,
as here suggested, for the Mausoleum.

† The ease with which the Knights got access to
this tomb would entirely contradict the supposition of
its being walled up, if it was the Tomb of Mausolus
they reached. It may have been that of the Queen.

stances there would be no difficulty in finding it a place, either in the long lacunaria at either end of the cella, or the shorter ones in the flanks, or in the square ones which are found at each angle of the building ; or, if none of these will do, one may be provided internally to suit any shape. There is, in fact, no direct evidence bearing on this subject ; but my impression is, that the arrangement of the roof, as suggested by the intercolumniation here adopted, must have been a singularly pleasing one. The four great lacunaria at the angles, being exactly square, would not only be very grand in themselves, but form a pleasing transition between the two other forms which ornament the flanks and front.

As all these points will be more easily understood by an inspection of the plans and sections, it is unnecessary to add more verbally about them here ; and it only remains to say a few words about the sculpture and the pedestals on which it stood, before concluding the description of the building.

Before doing so it may be as well to recapitulate some of the principal measures obtained from the preceding investigation.

Basing the whole on the width of the principal step, or 21 Greek inches, equal to 1 Babylonian cubit, we found 2 cubits, or 3 ft. 6 in., equal to the distance between one Lion's head and the next ; three Lions' heads, or 6 cubits, equal to one intercolumniation ; six intercolumniations, or 36 cubits, equal to 63 feet, or the length of the cella ; twice that, 126 feet, or 72 cubits, equal to the length of the lower step, which is also the height of the building without the quadriga. The lower step of the pyramid was 100 feet by 80, its spread 40 feet in one direction by 32 in the other, the meta 20 feet by 16—all in the ratio of 5 to 4 ; the cella internally, 42 feet by 52 ft. 6 in., or as 4 is to 5 ; externally, 52 ft. 6 in. by 63 ft., or as 5 is to 6—these three dimensions being in the ratio of 4, 5, and 6 ; the peristyle one intercolumniation on the flanks, one and a half in front. Measured transversely across the base, we found—

	Ft.	In.	Cubits.
For the width of the cella	42	0	or 24
Twice 21 for the width of the peristele is	42	0	„ 24
5 ft. 3 in. × 2 equal to 10 ft. 6 in. for the pedestals . . .	10	6	„ 6
5 ft. 3 in. × 2 „ „ for the steps	10	6	„ 6
Length of lower step	105	0	= 60

Lengthways we found—

	Ft.	In.	Cubits.
For the length of the cella	63	0	or 36
Width of the stairs or sepulchral chamber 21 ft. × 2 . . .	42	0	„ 24
Width of pedestals and steps as above	21	0	„ 12
Length of lower step	126	0	72*

* The building that most resembles the Mausoleum in design and dimensions among the products of modern art is probably the Arc de l'Etoile at Paris. Its length (rejecting fractions) is 150 feet English, its width 75. Its " totus circuitus " is therefore 450 as compared with the 416 of the Mausoleum. But, on the other hand, the area covered by the latter building is more than 2000 feet in excess of that covered by the former.

The total circumference, measured on the lower step, was—

		Feet.	Cubits.
126 feet, or 72 cubits × 2	=	252 or	144
105　　　　60　　　× 2	=	210	120
		462	264*

It is not necessary to say anything further with regard to the vertical heights. Till the system of definite proportions of the monument are more fully worked out than they can be in such a work as this, it will be better to adhere literally to Pliny's measurements as they stand in the text. They explain and fix all the vertical dimensions with sufficient precision for all practical purposes, though I cannot help suspecting that even he was wrong to the extent of an inch or two here or there, from not exactly understanding the subject he was treating. All this, however, is of no consequence in so far as the design is concerned, and therefore of secondary interest here.

Sculpture and Pedestals.

Of the three friezes that were found in the excavations, two are so similar that they were generally mistaken for parts of the same composition. The reasons, however, assigned by Mr. Newton for believing that they were different are so cogent as to leave very little doubt of the fact that they were so. The first of these, of which the Museum possesses 16 slabs, represents a combat of Amazons, and may therefore be called the Amazon frieze. The second, which is very similar, in like manner represents a combat of Lapithæ and Centaurs, and may therefore be called by their name. The last, which is in lower relief and less weather-worn, represents, principally at least, a chariot race.

The two first are so similar in dimensions and style that they were evidently parts of the same system of decoration. One, there can be little doubt, belonged to the order, the other to the basement; but there do not seem to be any sufficient data for ascertaining which; and, as it is not of the least consequence for the purposes of the restoration, I shall not enter upon the question at present. They are so similar in dimensions as well as in design and in relief that either may be taken.

The height of the Arc de l'Etoile is 150 feet to the cornice of the attic, and therefore considerably in excess, and it was intended to have been crowned with a quadriga, which, with its low pedestal, would have added 45 feet to this dimension, thus making up 195 feet as compared with 141·7, which was the total height of the Mausoleum. It is, however, one of the peculiarities and one of the principal beauties of the design of the Mausoleum, that it would have looked very much larger and probably even higher than the " Arc," had it occupied its situation ; and it is quite certain that a chariot group 14 feet high would look larger and more dignified on a pedestal raised on a pyramid, as at Halicarnassus, than would one twice that height on the great flat roof of the " Arc." In the one case the group compares with a base of 20 feet by 16, in the other with a great flat measuring 150 feet by 75. At Halicarnassus one-tenth of the whole height was quite sufficient for the crowning group; at Paris one-fifth would hardly have sufficed to produce the same effect.

* It may be accident, but it is a curious coincidence, that the number of feet read backwards gives the number of cubits,—the number of cubits read backwards, the number of feet.

To us, who only think of getting the full value of our money in whatever we do, it seems difficult to understand why so much labour and such careful art should have been bestowed on a frieze which was to be placed at a height of 80 feet from the spectator's eye.* But the Greeks slurred nothing, and seemed to have felt an innate satisfaction in knowing that a work was perfect and true, even if the eye could not grasp it, which must have been the case with many of the minuter proportional ratios which they considered so important.

In estimating this, we must not lose sight of the beauty of the climate and clearness of the atmosphere, which rendered things sharply visible at distances whence all would be hazy confusion in our grey atmosphere. Nor must we forget that all the principal features of the architecture were certainly accentuated by colour, and even if it is contended that the figures themselves were not painted, no one now hardly will deny that they were relieved by a painted background; and it is very difficult to believe that the colour could have stopped there. When new, the white marble, relieved and surrounded by coloured architecture, must have been a most painful and intolerable discord; and although the figures may not have been painted to look like life, it hardly seems doubtful but that the flesh was tinted and the robes coloured, at least to such an extent as to distinguish them, not only from the flesh, but from one another.

Traces of colour have been found on some of the bassi-rilievi of the Mausoleum. The lions certainly were painted, and with no sparing hand; and the colours found on the architecture were strong and distinct, as they generally are.

With such adjuncts and in such a climate, even at a distance of 80 feet, all the principal features of the frieze could easily have been distinguished, and the effect of it, in so far as we can judge, must have been something worthy of all the admiration lavished on this building.

The chariot-race frieze may either have been placed in one of the interior halls of the building, or it may have encircled the cella immediately under the roof, like the celebrated Panathenaic frieze of the Parthenon. On the doctrine of chances some fragments ought to have been found of the internal sculpture described by Guichard; and for myself I feel inclined to fancy this may be a part; but if not, its position was almost certainly the one hinted at just now, and shown in the plates.

The square tablets in like manner were also probably internal; but if not, their position would, I fancy, certainly be the back wall of the cella, under the peristyle. There being no windows there, some relief would be required, and these seem appropriate for the position, which is that suggested by Mr. Pullan; though he marred his suggestion by the position of his frieze, and by giving no access to either.

Besides these a considerable number of statues were found larger than life;

---

* The upper frieze of St. Paul's Cathedral is 95 feet from the ground.

namely, some 7 or 8 feet in height. These, following the suggestion of the Xanthian monument discovered by Sir Charles Fellows, I have placed in the peristele,—not the peristyle. I cannot fancy any position in which statues would either be more appropriate, or seen to greater advantage. Their dimensions require that they should be placed at some height above the eye. It is here 17 feet, and no niche could be better than the plain surface of the stele on either side, with the subdued shadow behind. In no building, ancient or modern, do I know any situation where statues would be so ádvantageous to the architecture, and on the other hand where the architecture would assist so advantageously in heightening the effect of the sculpture.*

In the tomb discovered by Mr. Falkener at Denzili, and which is evidently a copy of the Mausoleum, the pyramid is supported by just such a range of steles as have been introduced here, but with this curious peculiarity, that instead of the statues being placed between the piers, one is sculptured in mezzo rilievo on each face of the stele. The reason of this is obvious enough : there being no cella in that small monument (there are only 6 steles altogether), there would have been a strong light behind the statues and in the spectator's eyes, which would have rendered the expression of the statues invisible. As it is, it is one of those instances of intelligent copying so common in ancient and so rare in modern times.

We next come to the Lions. Fragments of some 20 of these were discovered. From their weather-worn appearance, and the general exigencies of the case, it is certain that they were placed on pedestals outside the building. There is no difficulty in providing these :—the design requires that there should be 7 such on the south, and as many on the north face of the building, each 5 feet 3 inches in length ; and 5 pedestals on the west, and 2 on the east, in like manner 5 ft. 3 in. long. These dimensions are exactly suited to the dimensions of the Lions found, which, as far as can be ascertained, were about 4 feet 6 inches long, from head to hind-quarter, though some seemed about 3 inches longer than the others, probably those on the longer faces of the building.

According to the evidence of Mr. Newton's book, all these were standing. As an architect I should have liked them better if they had been couchant, and it seems probable that some at least were sitting. Two are represented in that attitude in the Dilettante Society's plate of the Castle at Budrum, and I cannot help thinking that a more careful examination would show an attitude of more repose in the others. In all that concerns sculpture, however, I bow to Mr. Newton's authority, and accept the facts as he states them. Their being standing seems to necessitate pedestals for the statues of the peristele, which otherwise it might have been better to have dispensed with. Taking them

---

* In St. George's Hall, Liverpool, the architect provided situations for statues in nearly a similar manner. As compared with these, the defects of his arrangement are that the spaces are too large and the shadows behind not deep enough.

either as sitting, standing, or couchant, they give life to and relieve the base-ment to a very great extent.

Besides these 21 I have added two Lions of larger size on each side of the portal, where the larger pedestals seem to require their presence. These I have made couchant, their length thus ranging with the standing lions on either side.

I have also taken the liberty of suggesting 4 couchant lions on pedestals at the 4 angles of the roof. The authority for this suggestion is the monument at Dugga (Woodcut, No. 2), where four corner stones cut into the pyramidal roof at the angles in this manner, and were evidently surmounted by sculpture or ornament of some similar character; but more than this, I feel that something is necessary here in order to support the central pedestal that carried the quadriga. Without this it would look isolated and hardly a part of the general design. Besides this, the grouping of the columns at the angles seems to suggest something of the sort, while on the other hand an architect would probably introduce some such arrangement in order to justify the grouping.

Altogether these roof pedestals seem to me so essential to the design that I have no hesitation in saying I believe they must have been there; but as there has been nothing found to suggest them,—though nothing either to contradict their existence,—the suggestion must be taken only for what it is worth, and it is quite open to any one to say that he thinks them superfluous.

Having proceeded so far with the restoration, it is found that there are two pedestals at each angle waiting for occupants. These measure each 12 feet in front, by 5 ft. 3 in. on the sides. When I first found these dimensions, it struck me that they were those of the pedestals of the celebrated Monte Cavallo groups, and finding on inquiry that I was correct in this, I jumped at once to the con-clusion that these beautiful sculptures once adorned this wonder of the world! Personally I am still inclined to adhere to this opinion, but I feel so little competent to decide such a question that I have not introduced them in the perspective restoration, though I have suggested them on Plate II., and shall await with interest the opinions of others on the subject.

There can be no doubt but that they belong to the age of the Mausoleum and no one seems to know where they came from, while the arrangement of the group is certainly very peculiar (Woodcut, No. 6). It is true it is quite impossible that the angle line of the building could have been lost behind such a pedestal as this; and the two, if belonging to the Mausoleum, must have stood on separate pedestals; but this I think would have been an improvement; certainly so in that situation; but when placed where no architectural exigencies suggested their arrangement, nothing could be so easy as to bring them together as we now find them by simply sawing through their pedestals on the dotted line. At all events the coincidence is

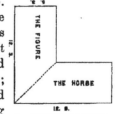

6.—PEDESTAL OF MONTE CAVALLO GROUP.

most remarkable, and it is also a curious coincidence that Cicero should accuse Verres of robbing Halicarnassus of its statues. Why not of these? We know how Mummius plundered Corinth more than a century before that time. There seems no inherent improbability in the case.

Assuming for the moment that these sculptures came from the Mausoleum, there is no reason to suppose that there ever were more than two such groups, and they would therefore have adorned the southern face, and the figures would in consequence have been the work of Timotheus. There would consequently be still four pedestals, which were almost certainly occupied by men or Amazons on horseback, such as the torso in the Museum, which is avowedly the most beautiful thing which was found in the excavations. These pedestals, both from their position and size, are just such as are required for this kind of sculpture, and such as would show it off to the greatest advantage. The one question seems to be, were all the eight pedestals adorned with similar sculptures, or were four occupied by the Monte Cavallo groups, and four by the prancing Amazons? *

It only now remains to refer to one of Pliny's dimensions, which could not be explained till these pedestals and their uses were established. The great puzzle of his description always was, that with the dimensions given for other parts, the "totus circuitus" should be 411 feet. This is evidently no loose measurement or mere guess, but a dimension copied out of the book of the architects, and unless it can be absolutely incorporated with the design, no restoration can for one moment be allowed to pass muster. The plain meaning, as I understand it, is that this was the girth of the building; it is such a measurement as a man would take of the bole of a tree, or, in other words, of any object of which he wished to know what the length of a tape or rope would be which he could bind round it,—in this instance on the upper step.

Turning to the plan (Plate I.) and to the measurements (page 37), we find the north and south faces measure 105 Greek feet, the east and west 84 feet— together, 378 feet; each angle measures across 7 ft. 6 in., and adding this 30 feet to the above, we obtain the total of 408, or 3 feet too short. This slight difference, however, is easily accounted for. That dimension is taken over the waist of the pedestals, and by allowing 4 inches for the projection of the plinth, which is a very probable amount of projection, we get the exact dimension of 411 feet we are seeking for, as measured on the upper step of the building, which is where we should naturally look for it. Not only, therefore, does this offer no difficulty, but it is a most satisfactory confirmation of all that has been urged before.

---

* In the perspective drawing forming the title-page, these pedestals seem to break up the base of the building too much. If seen more in front either way this effect would have been avoided. As explained above, the dimensions necessitate a projection between the top step and the face of the peristele of 5·3. This must either have been a shelf or broken up as here suggested. I cannot conceive that it was the former for many obvious reasons, while the latter seems to me not only appropriate architecturally, but to be indispensable to the display of the sculpture. They exactly fulfil the part that is performed by the buttresses in Gothic architecture.

CONCLUSION.

On some future occasion it may be worth while to go more fully into all the minor details of this important building, and to illustrate it to a greater extent than has been attempted in this short treatise ; not only because it was the building which the ancients, who ought to have been the best judges, admired most of all their architectural treasures, but because it is the one which illustrates best the principles on which their great buildings were designed.

It might, therefore, be well worth while to treat it as a typical example and use it to illustrate not only the principles of Greek design in general, but more particularly to explain the doctrine of harmonic proportions in accordance with which they all were designed, and of which it is, in so far as we at present know, the most perfect example the knowledge of which has come down to our times.

All that has been attempted on the present occasion is, to point out the main broad features of harmonic proportion which governed the principal dimensions of the building ; but the " order " was also full of minute and delicate harmonies worthy of the most intense study. To elucidate these something more is required than a hap-hazard restoration, such as that which is found in the plates attached to Mr. Newton's work, with the superinduced confusion of the lithographers' inaccuracies. Every fragment requires re-examination, and every part re-measurement ; but to do this requires not only unlimited access to the remains, but power to move and examine, which would not, of course, be granted, to me at least. But if it were done, and if the details were published, with the really good specimens of the sculpture, all of which are omitted from Mr. Newton's present publication, the public might then come to understand what the Mausoleum really was, and why the ancients admired it so much.

The building is also especially interesting, because it is more complicated in its parts and more nearly approaches the form of civil architecture than anything that has yet come to our knowledge. Almost all the Greek buildings hitherto explored are Temples, generally formal and low in their outline. For the first time, we find a genuine two-storied building, which, though covering only half the area of the Parthenon, is twice its height, and contains a variety of lessons and suggestions it would be in vain to try to extract from mere templar buildings.

This building seems also to have a special interest at the present moment, inasmuch as we are now looking everywhere for the design of some Memorial which should worthily commemorate the virtues of the Prince whose loss the nation is still deploring. It would be difficult to suggest anything more appropriate for this purpose than a reproduction of the Monument which excited so much the admiration of the ancient world, and rendered the grief of Artemisia famous through all succeeding generations.

LONDON:
PRINTED BY W. CLOWES AND SONS, STAMFORD STREET,
AND CHARING CROSS.

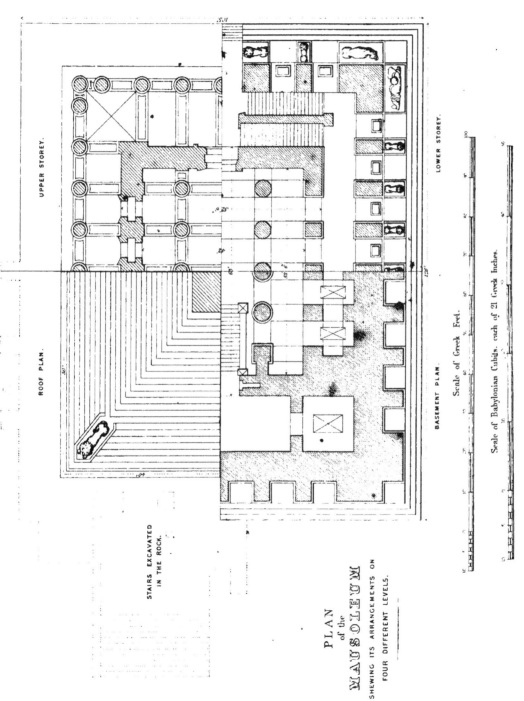

PLAN
of the
MAUSOLEUM.
SHEWING ITS ARRANGEMENTS ON
FOUR DIFFERENT LEVELS.

ROOF PLAN.

UPPER STOREY.

STAIRS EXCAVATED
IN THE ROCK.

BASEMENT PLAN.

LOWER STOREY.

Scale of Greek Feet.

Scale of Babylonian Cubits, each of 21 Greek Inches.

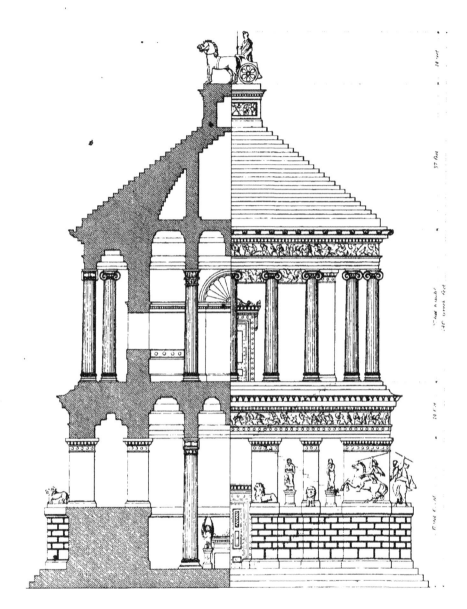

HALF SECTION.   HALF ELEVATION.

EAST FRONT OF MAUSOLEUM.

Scale of Greek Feet.

Scale of Babylonian Cubits each of 21 Greek Inches.

PLATE III.

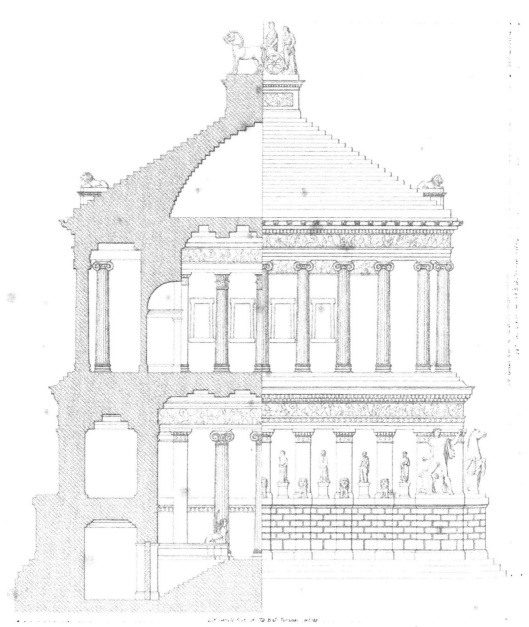

HALF SECTION.   HALF ELEVATION.

SOUTH SIDE OF MAUSOLEUM.

Scale of Greek Feet.

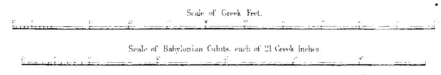

Scale of Babylonian Cubits, each of 21 Greek Inches.

J. FERGUSSON DEL.   JOHN MURRAY, ALBEMARLE ST. LONDON.

CPSIA information can be obtained at www.ICGtesting.com
Printed in the USA
BVOW09s0656050915

416623BV00020B/842/P

9 781276 558143